Interview

Best Answers to Tough Questions for Total Confidence

Table of Contents

Chapter 1:

First Impressions Count

Today there are few jobs that do not require the candidates to first have at least one interview, and for more senior positions there may be several interviews before the position is finally awarded. My daughter has just picked up a part time, minimum wage job to supplement her pocket money during her final year at school and even at that low entry level she was first given a full interview where in years gone by a simple chat with the manager may have sufficed.

For many people, even the thought of being interviewed may bring on an attack of nerves and a sickening feeling deep in their stomachs. This book sets out to alleviate those feelings of fear so that you are able to handle any interview with confidence, safe in the knowledge of what you need to do in order not only to answer the questions that will be thrown at you, but also to use them as platforms from which to demonstrate why you are the best candidate for the position.

While the interview may be an intimidating process to go through, always bear in mind that it also offers you an opportunity to get a close up look at the company who is conducting the interview. Being interviewed is a two way street and just as the company that is interviewing you is looking for their ideal candidate; you too are looking for the ideal position that blends both your skills and your choice of a satisfying work environment.

The saying goes 'you do not get a second chance to make a good first impression' and that is never truer than when attending a job interview. Whether you are being assessed by a panel, or just by one individual, much of the way in which you are perceived will be as a result of the aura you give off before you have even uttered one word. Whilst you do not have an exact idea of how the interview will proceed in terms of questions and format, you do know that the first impression you present will be crucially important. This is basic common sense and there is no excuse for you not to hit this one out of the ballpark. It is extraordinary how many people blow their shot at a good first impression simply because they have not put in the effort and thought as to how they will be perceived by their interviewers. Whilst a lax first impression might not be a deal breaker it certainly means that you will be coming from behind and there is just no excuse for this.

How to dress

Once upon a time there was an unstated but universally accepted rule that you dressed formally for an interview. In many jobs these days that is no longer a requirement but virtually every profession or job has some form of dress code. It might not be written in a rulebook but it will exist and you need to find out what it is. If all the employees are wearing conservative suits and ties then you should be wearing a suit and tie. If the code is smart casual then likewise you need to be smart and casual.

Some people may feel that this infringes on their individuality and that they should be hired for their abilities rather than their appearance. Now is not the time to start getting on your high horse about your rights and your freedoms. You are trying to get hired, not make a politically correct statement and if the dress code is not to your liking then you should have picked this up whilst researching the company and not applied for that position.

Before entering the room

Often before a job interview you will find yourself in a waiting room or lobby where there may be several other candidates. This can be a time when fear levels expand as you mind starts to run through all the disaster scenarios it can come up with. Now is when you need to feed yourself with positive self-images and go through a quick checklist to ensure that all is as ready as you can make it. If there is a receptionist greeting you or checking you in, then treat them warmly and with respect. They can be great allies and are often overlooked in the tense waiting period before an interview. Don't assume that the interviewer will not ask for their impression of the interviewees after you have left. If you are chewing gum, lose it; if you cell phone is turned on, turn it off. Hopefully you have been forward thinking enough to bring extra

2

copies of your resume in case there is more than one interviewer. If not there is an outside chance you can talk the receptionist into making a quick couple of copies for you but be sensitive about this and don't even try if it looks like it will cause offence.

Attitude

This waiting period is a great time to do a few deep breathing exercises and make some positive reinforcement statements to you. Focus on the positive and try to induce feelings of self-confidence. Our minds play a crucial role in so much that it is worth learning some positive thinking techniques so that you enter that interview room with nothing but positive thoughts about both yourself and the interview process. Your mental attitude impacts on your confidence, your demeanor and even the way you carry yourself. A period of waiting can boil up into a time of nervousness but if managed well it can just as easily give you a chance to gather your thoughts and instill a feeling of calmness. Drown out any negative thoughts that pop up by replacing them with positive, self-affirming ones.

Body language

From the moment you step into the interview room you are being assessed. How you are dressed, how you carry yourself and how you present yourself to others all count. Introduce yourself, carry yourself with poise and confidence and above all make eye contact and smile. Smiling makes you more likeable and likability plays a big part in all areas of human interaction.

Whatever feelings you may have inside of you should be disregarded in favor of the image you want to portray. Poised self-confidence must be all that can be seen from the outside. When you are seated then sit upright and with your body squarely facing the interviewer. Make eye contact during communication and use that smile whenever possible. It will boost your likeability but will also help you to relax more. As the interview progresses don't allow yourself to slump down or adopt a more curled up defensive looking posture, even if the questions are tough. Keep telling yourself you were made for this job and that you have all the requisite skills to do it well. Don't allow the questions to throw your equilibrium. In a panicked state, the most common reaction is to try to demonstrate your knowledge by answering quickly. Instead take your time to let the question sink in and make sure that you know what it is that you are really being asked. There is a fine line between being reflective and looking like you are trying to make something up, but remember this is not a first to the buzzer quiz and the interviewers genuinely want to hear your thoughts. If you don't understand a question then ask for clarification rather than make up and answer to a question you have not understood. More about that in the next chapter.

Chapter 2:

What the Interviewer is Looking For?

One of the best ways to overcome the fear of being interviewed is to put oneself in the interviewer's shoes for a while. Firstly, he or she is looking to fill a specific position and their primary goal is not to trip you up or coerce you into making a fool of yourself. In many cases they may well be working closely with you after the interview if you are deemed to be the right candidate and that is the reason that likability that I mentioned in the previous chapter is so important.

Their role is not only to find out if you have the requisite skills to perform the tasks that the job entails, but it is also to establish whether or not you have what it takes to fit the company profile. There is little point in hiring a candidate who is so at odds with all the other employees that there are likely to be personality clashes somewhere down the line. Once they are satisfied that you are a comfortable fit for their organization they will need to move on to assessing if you are capable of doing the job that you are applying for. This is where it is important to have done your homework before the interview.

Know what you are applying for

Before attending an interview you need to have mined every possible source of information to know not only what the job is about but also what the company is about. It is all too common for applicants to arrive at an interview with total confidence in their qualifications and the power of their resumes but little underlying knowledge of the philosophy of that particular company. There is little point in coming across as an accountant capable of squeezing every cent of profit out of an organization if that organization has the job satisfaction of its staff as one of its highest priorities. You will need to know those priorities and tailor your interview technique, and perhaps even your resume, to those values that the company holds most dear.

The person conducting the interview will have in depth knowledge of the philosophy of the company. They may even have been instrumental in creating it. When doing the interview they will lean toward the candidate who most fits the company persona. What is more, they may not even know they are doing so. So whilst having the best qualifications is important, there is little that can be done to change those at this late stage. Aligning yourself with the way the company perceives itself may just give you the edge over someone with better qualifications but who is not seen as being a 'good fit'.

In many cases the interviewer is looking at you as a person rather than your skill set. From your resume he knows what skills you have and he may have a dozen other applicants with similar skills or qualifications. He or she needs to assess you and your ability to use those skills within the company context rather than the skills themselves. This is a crucial point that so many people being interviewed miss. They brush up on their particular field of expertise but neglect to get an in depth knowledge of the specific requirements of the job and what the company focus really is.

For the candidate who prepares well this provides an opportunity to shine. Sure you have the qualifications, but you also know where the company hopes to go, what it has in the way of priorities and what issues it faces or has faced in the past. It has never been easier to research an organization than it is today with the Internet and company reporting rules. Even with these tools available there is still little to beat that good old, first hand information. If you know somebody in the company, or somebody that knows somebody in the company, it is a great idea to take that person out for a drink and gather the in depth knowledge you simply would not be able to obtain other than from the inside. If you get an opportunity like this then grab it.

Even with the right qualifications and a really good idea of the company ethos you need to expect the interviewer to ask some tough questions. We will look at some of these in greater depth later in the book but what you need to understand is that even if these questions appear somewhat aggressive or irrelevant, what the interviewer is doing is trying to see how you handle pressure. You should not see this as an attack or act of provocation on yourself personally. Just stay calm, take your time and try to assess what the questioner is really trying to find out rather than allowing yourself to simply react. In many cases, even if an answer to a difficult question is wrong, the fact that is delivered with confidence and in a calm manner will augur well for the candidate. Bear in mind that in some cases there is no right or wrong answer and that the question is asked purely to assess your response. If you feel that is the case just be true to yourself and your own beliefs rather than attempting to second-guess what the deeper meaning behind the question might be.

Chapter 3:

Being Interviewed is a Skill That Can be Learned

For most people living in the modern business environment, the days of having just one job from the time you leave college to the day you retire are over. According to the Bureau of Labor Statistics, the average worker now has ten jobs before the age of forty and that number is likely to increase. Overall, in the US, a worker can expect to go through fourteen interviews before landing a position and in Europe and the United Kingdom that figure is not much smaller. That equates to one hundred and forty interviews just until the age of forty. With the retirement age getting pushed back more and more as we struggle to make ends meet, many people will continue to work until well into their sixties and that means yet more interviews. All in all, this equates to a huge number of interviews over the course of a life time and that means that being interviewed is a skill that we are going to have to develop if we do not want to find ourselves going through long periods of unemployment with all the mental and financial problems that that can bring.

Being interviewed is a skill and like any skill it can be developed and honed with practice. Try watching a celebrity when they are interviewed about the latest blockbuster movie that they have just starred in. Prior to release they will go through dozens of these interviews and it is clear that they have a very good idea of what questions they are likely to be asked and what the best replies to those questions are. They know exactly when to smile and when to give that sad empathetic little grimace. They are not able to perform this simply because of some gift that lies in their genes. Instead, experienced public relations experts whose job it is to anticipate the questions and help them develop the correct responses have carefully prepped them.

You too are going to need to hone your skills and anticipate questions that will be fired at you. A good way to practice is to have someone you trust interview you. It will need to be someone that will be brutally honest and who perhaps has some experience in conducting interviews. Give them permission to make the practice sessions far reaching so that you gain experience at answering a broad range of questions. After the dummy interview get some honest feedback and not just about how you responded but also about your demeanor, body language and eye contact. Adjust accordingly.

Of course there is no substitute for the real thing so go to as many interviews as possible and treat each of them as a method to improve your technique. You may even want to make notes afterwards as to how you performed and where you felt your weaknesses lay. Do not limit yourself to applying only for your ideal position. Aim wide and tackle each interview with as much enthusiasm and passion as you would that dream job. If all you gain is confidence and a better-developed technique that will serve you I the future. There is always the possibility that you may learn something about the position that you had not realized and suddenly you may find yourself actually wanting the job. Also you are exposing yourself to people in the business of hiring and if you are good they may see something in you that they could use in a different position, possibly one that has not yet been advertised. This is yet another reason that every interview must be tackled with all the seriousness and enthusiasm that you would bring to an interview for that dream job. Even for experienced candidates, lack of enthusiasm shows and that is something that can very quickly kill the desire to hire a person.

Chapter 4:

Refining Your Life Story

Any interviewer worth his salt is going to want to find out more about you and what makes you tick. It is all very well knowing what you are capable of with regards to your qualifications and ability to perform a certain function, but there is always an element of human interest. He or she will want to know something deeper than just what you can do. They will want to know who you are.

The trouble is that many of us believe we lead totally boring lives and that there is nothing about us that warrants any further attention. When it comes to an interview, this is the wrong sort of thinking. You must work on the assumption that somewhere during the interview you will be asked something about who you are and you must have an answer ready and waiting. This question may seem irrelevant; small talk even, but it presents you with a huge opportunity to shine and make yourself memorable.

Each of us has our own unique story. We have not all followed the same paths or done the same things. Our backgrounds are as different as our tastes in color or the books we choose to read. Human nature dictates that we are interested in other people's lives and when at an interview you are asked a seemingly mundane question about your seemingly mundane life then be sure to grab that opportunity. You are able to present something unique here. Something none of the other ten candidates sitting out in the waiting room can offer. This is a moment made just for you.

Like so many other parts of the interview process your chances of success are augmented dramatically if you have prepared. You need to have thought about your life and cherry picked what is of interest. It need not be an entire autobiography. You are only going to have a few seconds here, but this needs to be a few seconds that will make you stick in the interviewers mind. He might be conducting dozens of interviews each day and unless you can give him some handle to hang onto, your face is just going to be one more in that cloudy blur of faces that have sat across the desk from him during the course of his day.

This lesson was brought home to me many years ago. I sat for an interview in which the candidate ahead of me was interviewed for half an hour. My interview lasted less than five minutes. I later learned that the other candidate had researched the client and found that he had an interest in a certain hobby. During the first minute of that interview he had been able to mention that he had an interest in the same subject and for the remainder of the interview the two of them had talked of little else. It was classic demonstration of the advantages of preparation.

I am not suggesting that you go to the trouble of finding out the personal interests of every interviewer that you will be confronted by during the course of your lifetime. What I am advocating is that you have some snippets of your life story available that you can use to engage others with when the opportunity offers itself.

You may think you lead an incredibly uneventful life but if you sit down and edit it you will find that there are gems in your history that people would find either interesting or amusing. Look at your hobbies, any travel you may have done, photos from your past and even go through your sent emails. Somewhere in there are things that would be of interest to others. Pick out all those gems and go through them one by one, then start to edit the story of you. What is there that makes you amusing, brave, competent or compassionate. Perhaps you climbed a mountain and broke your ankle; perhaps you had measles as a kid and then infected the whole class. You may be a keen parachutist or have read a great book. No one can weave this story but you. It is yours alone but you cannot afford to answer the question with a pathetic shrug and an "Oh I don't do much really." For just a few minutes you have an opportunity to tell a short but fascinating story. Tell it.

Think of what you are trying to demonstrate here. In just a few sentences you need to show that you are human, that you have a unique aspect to you character that is yours alone and that you are able to connect at more than just a business level.

You can re-edit your life. It may sound somewhat manipulative but the fact is we all have many different facets to our lives and at an interview there will be certain facets that you want to show more than others. For example if you are interviewing for a job working with disabled people you may want to mention some aspect that demonstrates that you are a compassionate person. On the other hand if you are interviewing for a position in sales with a sports company you may get an opportunity to shine a light on the fact that you are a committed mountain bike enthusiast. You might be both compassionate and sporting but you have chosen to demonstrate that aspect that is most appropriate for the situation.

In weaving your life story together you will discover something about yourself that was there all along but the value of which you had simply overlooked. In doing this navel gazing exercise you might come away with increased self-confidence and possibly several different short scripts that could be used in different ways according to the circumstance.

Chapter 5:

Some Common Killer Questions

It is not possible to anticipate every question that might be thrown at you during the course of an interview. There are, however, a number of questions that generally crop up and if you read through this chapter you should have a much better appreciation of how to handle them. They will, of course, not come up word for word as they appear in the list below but instead will take on differing guises. Their exact wording is not important. What is important is that once you have read them you see the reasoning behind them. This will enable you to adapt your own replies and answer with the confidence that will impress the interviewer.

What is it about yourself that makes you the right candidate for this position?

This question pops up in one form or another in just about any interview. If the interviewee is not prepared for it they can be left fumbling for words but if they are prepared it opens the door for them to put their best foot forward and propose, smoothly and elegantly, all the reasons that the job should be theirs. Be careful though. Tone is very important and you should sound confident and knowledgeable but not come over as being arrogant.

Why do you want this job?

This should be a question you have already asked yourself and so it should be easy to roll out a short list of reasons why you have applied for this position. At the same time you can carefully phrase your answers so that they demonstrate a match between your talents and your reasons for applying for the job. Keep the list short and do not try to impress the interviewer by having the longest list he has ever heard.

What strengths do you possess that will make you good for this position?

Again this is a gift of a question if you have prepared for it. Don't just provide a long list of attributes that you think the employer may be looking for. Pick three or four of qualities you may have that are pertinent to the position and expand briefly on each of them.

What are your greatest weaknesses?

Another typical question and rarely left out by interviewers, this can be a kind of a trap that you create for yourself to fall into. Beware of it. While weaknesses are inherent in humans, you must prepare yourself to present it well and in a dignified manner. Another way of talking about your weakness is telling stories from your past experience wherein you learnt from your mistakes and have since limited that particular weakness.

Also, when talking about persistent weaknesses, do NOT leave out how you manage and keep these negativities under check and how you ensure that they do not affect your professional life. Having weaknesses is a perfectly natural human trait, but not being aware of them, not accepting them and not planning to keep them under check is clearly unprofessional.

What is you greatest professional achievement?

Be careful here. In your working career you will hopefully have done several things that you are proud of. Don't just dive in with the things that pleased you the most. Instead pick the one that would most have benefitted the company that you are applying to now had you done something similar for them and expound on that.

What is your greatest personal achievement?

This is a question that allows the interviewer to get a chance to know a little more about you as a person. At the same time it is an occasion to show them something about yourself that they may not get to see anywhere else during the course of the interview. Have a few carefully chosen personal events at your finger tips and use the one that you feel will be most appropriate and will demonstrate some positive aspect of your character that they might not otherwise get to see. The life story that you have been editing from the previous chapter comes into play perfectly here.

Where do you see yourself in 2/5/10 years?

This can be a tricky one to deal with. You need to appear ambitious without being unreasonable. Of course if this job is just something you intend to do for a couple of years because you need it on your CV before moving onto bigger things then don't mention that. Be prepared, if that is the case, for the fact that they may have had other people use the position as a springboard to greater things and be using this as a question to test that you will not quickly be moving on.

Tell me about your dream job?

Here is a chance to describe the job you are applying for and building into it all the positive things you bring with you that match that position.

What other companies have you worked for?

They probably already know most of this from looking at your application. This question gives them an opportunity to find out what you did in those companies and your reasons for leaving. Keep everything positive and don't make disparaging remarks about any of the companies that have employed you in the past even if you had some sort of dispute.

Why did you leave your last position?

This often follows the question above. Even if you left your last employer after a stand up shouting match with your boss, keep your answer positive and don't bad mouth the company or anyone that you worked for or with whilst there. Instead focus more on the idea that you felt you needed to spread your wings more and that you had learned as much as you were going to in the last company but that you had really gained from that learning experience.

Have you ever been fired?

This can be a real hot potato of a question if you have been fired. Many industries are quite small and, like small villages, everyone knows a bit about everyone else's business so this question may have been posed simply to get your side of the story. If you were fired legitimately for gross misconduct or some similar issue and the interviewer is likely to know then the best approach may be to come clean and act contrite. Mention that you have learned from your mistake and are looking to start again with a clean slate. On the other hand if you were fired unfairly you are really going to need to be careful about how you answer. The opportunity to rant about injustice is something we all look for but this is not the right stage for it. Very calmly and briefly explain the reasons you were fired and why you believe that was incorrect or unfair. If you are pursuing litigation then you need to explain this in a manner that demonstrates that you feel unjustly treated but are not someone who litigates against a former employer without very good reason.

What work environment most suits you?

Hopefully you know what sort of environment you will be working in through the research that you have done. This is a time to reel off all the things that the new position already offers in the way of a work environment. As an addition, you may throw in one or two new ideas that would bring something positive to the position you are hoping to fill.

What would you describe as your management style?

As mentioned earlier in the book each company has its own style and ethic and hopefully you have a clear idea of the style that is already being used. Whilst you need to conform to any boundary that that imposes, you also need to be true to yourself. If the company is a hard hitting, authoritarian type organization and you have more of a team approach you might want to word things along the lines of "strict but open to ideas".

How did you hear about this position?

This shows the interviewer one of two things: where his job advertising revenue is being most effective or if you know someone in the company. If it is the latter then you might be able to name drop to show you already have friends in the company. If it is the former, don't just mention the source of your information. Instead turn this question into another opportunity by saying something to the effect that you were looking for a job exactly like the one you are applying for and after asking around you learned that the company placed its adds in that particular area.

What is your educational background?

The interviewer will have a basic idea from your CV but now you have been given an open door to expand on that whilst emphasizing what you deem the most positive aspects of your education.

Describe yourself?

This trips up so many people who are not expecting the question but it is a gift for those who are prepared for it. Of course you are not going to say "I am an alcoholic who sleeps late most days and likes to kick his dog after a night on the town." The questioner has just given you a chance to highlight anything constructive about your own character that pertains to the job you are going for. Don't go off tangent by talking about all the good things you did as a Boy Scout but filter down the positive things that would benefit the company if they employed you. Also remember that you have been asked to describe yourself and not just what is positive about yourself. Throw in a few negatives but turn them to demonstrate that you have adopted positive strategies to correct them.

What is your biggest failure?

Another question that can prove a real landmine if you have not thought it through beforehand. You need to have some sort of failure in your past to mention here and we all have plenty of those. Don't follow the question to the letter by presenting the worst one. Instead choose a situation that went really badly for you but which you have now turned around to enhance your life. What the failure was does not really matter. What counts is that you were able to take a negative situation and turn it into a positive one in some way.

What is the name of our CEO?

You better know this one. Simply do a Google search for the name of the CEO before the interview begins.

What are your hobbies?

An easy question that allows you to show something about your personal life. If you aren't involved in a hobby that other people might find interesting you might want to think about taking one up.

How would you feel about firing someone you work with?

Ouch! In some jobs there are going to be times when you need to get rid of somebody. Don't ever make this look like something that you would take lightly or do if you did not have to. You need to show that you have what it takes to do what needs to be done but that you do so only with the greatest of reluctance and after much consideration.

How do you handle pressure?

Some people handle pressure easily and even a question like this poses no problem to them. Others struggle when under pressure. If you are one of those who struggle when pressurized you need to tread carefully when answering this question. Firstly you do not want to appear to be a person who will cave in and burst into tears at the slightest sign of a problem. You also don't want to take on a job where the stress levels are going to be so high that you are unable to cope. Some sort of middle ground is needed here and you need to have a good idea of the strain that the job will put you under. If you will not be able to cope then do not apply. If you can then talk confidently about what you are capable of to show the interviewer that the stresses the job will create do not bother you.

Who do you most admire?

So many people miss a great opportunity with this gift question. Most will mention the obvious characters like Bill Gates or President Obama. This is fine except it puts the ball right back in the hands of the person who is conducting the interview. He has also heard those same names a dozen times when interviewing for the position you want.

Researching a little on biographies will expose you to thousands of inspirational characters you can be sure the interviewer has never heard of. Find one that has a really interesting story and a big character and then throw that name in. The interviewer is bound to ask who the person is and why you admire them and this then gives you a chance to hold court on some of the interesting and admirable things that person has done to warrant your admiration. You have just made yourself stand out from the crowd with very little effort.

Do you see yourself as a leader? Why?

Of course you do. What is more you have once again been given a perfect opportunity to point to all those powerful qualities you possess that the interviewer may not have picked up on had you not taken him there. Make sure you show that your leadership qualities are balanced and fair and do not come across as a dictator in the making.

Who are our competitors?

From your research you should have been able to pick up the answer to this one. It would be in your own interests to find out, as you might want to apply for a job with them in the event of not being the chosen candidate in the present interview.

Why are you looking to change positions?

As with many other questions this gives you the chance to show that you are ambitious and also that you have researched the company you are interviewing for and have found things there that attract you toward a position in that company.

What salary are you looking for?

Be clear but realistic as to your worth in the market place. Avoid underselling yourself for fear that you will not get the job. If you secure a position on the grounds of a salary that is below what you want you run a very real risk of resentment setting in down the line. At the same you don't want to lose the job simply because you make a grab for too much money.

List your strengths?

This is just the same question as many of the others but posed in a slightly different way. You should see it as an opportunity to show some of the strengths that you will be able to bring to the company. Rather than simply rattling off a long list of everything positive you can possibly come up with, focus just on three of them. Expand on each one and show how and why you see yourself as strong in those particular areas and what experience you have. A short list with in depth reasoning will have more force than a long undeveloped list.

What is it that most motivates you?

We are all motivated by different things. So is the company, which you are now hoping to join. Try to make sure that your motivations are in line with those of the company but at the same time don't become so focused on being what you think they want you to be that you lose sight of who you really are and fail to be true to yourself.

Are you a team player?

You probably will not be asked this question if you are being interviewed for the position of lighthouse keeper on some remote island. The answer to this question should be yes but you will need to back this up with examples from your past jobs and possibly even from your personal life. If you play a team sport now is the time to mention it. If you participated in any team building activities during your past working life then expand on those.

What constitutes a good team player?

A good team player needs to have many different qualities including the ability to get on with others, offer positive feedback and sometimes overlook things that might cause unnecessary tension. You must show that you understand all the facets of team playing, as this will be an important factor in the hiring procedure.

Tell me about your experience in this field?

Think of this as an opportunity to show the interviewer that you understand what team playing consists of and that you have a broad experience in this area.

What are your hobbies?

When he asks this question the interviewer is not really trying to find out what your hobbies are. He is really trying to see what kind of person you are and find out what motivates and stimulates you. This question gives you a blank canvass to stand out if you handle it well. Even if your only hobby is learning to play the harmonica it offers a chance to show off your human side; how you persevere despite the difficulty, have made friends in the field and gives a chance to add some humorous incident that may have taken place as you learn. If you have prepared for this question it should be easy to expose a side of your character that may make all the difference between getting a job and not getting one.

Tell me about your family?

Companies like to imagine that their staff lives in a constant state of happy family bliss. Don't use this as a chance to vent your spleen about getting cut out of great aunty Jane's will or to pour out your complaints about your ex failing to deliver on monthly maintenance payments. The interviewer is not your therapist so just tell him what he wants to hear. You do not want to give the impression that you will be taking days off to deal with family problems either.

Tell me about a conflict you had in your last/present job and how you dealt with it?

Another ouch question but one that can be transformed in your favor if you handle it well. You are bound to have had some sort of conflict in your work life but present one that is relatively minor and most of all has a happy outcome after you dealt with it. This will be difficult to come up with if you have not prepared for it in advance.

Tell me about a conflict you have had with your boss?

This is a very sensitive subject. If you have not had a conflict with your boss you can easily side step any problem but if you have had a conflict and it is possible that the interviewer may be aware of that then you better be ready to deal with this question. Try to quickly change the wording from 'conflict' to the less aggressive 'disagreement'. Point out that though you may have had a different opinion to your boss you were able to amicably resolve this and concede that your boss was right if that was the case.

Are you ambitious?

Ambition is not something to be ashamed of and can be beneficial to a company as it produces motivation.

What are your ambitions?

The ambitions you admit to here need to fit within the constraints of the job you are applying for. If you wish to get ahead in the company then state this but if you want to gain some experience before going out on your own in two or three years time then you might want to keep that under your hat. A company does not want to feel that it is only acting as a training ground for people on their way to bigger things.

What comes first, family or work?

This question is a bit of a booby trap. It is tempting, when desperately hoping for a job, to dive right in and say that you would put the company before any other interest but that is unlikely and the interviewer will know that. Be honest and tell them that although the job would be very important to you in an emergency scenario you would need to think of your family's well being and weigh up what would be best both for them and the company. Mention that part of the well being of the family is related to the well being of the company and therefore both would have to be considered. A reasonable employer will accept this and if not you need to consider if you really want to be working for a company that would expect you to place your family second.

If we need to transfer you to another town/state/country how would you react?

This is probably not a trick question. If you are asked this you are probably applying for a position where there is a real possibility that you may be required to make a move. You need to be honest here because if you say you are happy to relocate you will be expected to honor that commitment. If this does not fit with your plans then state that up front. It is possible that there might be a position that would not require you to move but you do not want to find yourself taking on a job and then having to leave again because you refused a transfer when called upon to take one.

Chapter 6:

Off the Wall Questions

The questions that we looked at in the previous chapter are questions that you might come across in many an average interview. If you can deal with them with confidence then you give your interview prospects a massive boost. These days many employers have started to expand their range of questions with some that seem to come from nowhere and appear to have little relevance either to you, the company or the job for which you are applying. With questions like who would win a fight between Spiderman and Batman? or how many ten cent coins would it take to fill a Boeing 747 airliner? it is impossible to really prepare for these in the way you might for those in the previous chapter.

Though you might think the interviewer has wandered totally off the reservation with questions like these, the fact is they are actually very clever. They give the interviewer a chance to get a real look at you as a person, to see if you think can your toes and to gain a better idea of whether or not you have a character that blends with that of the company. While there is probably no right answer there are definitely several wrong answers and "I don't know." or "I am not sure." are just two examples. You need to say something smart or funny and you need to have already assessed your interviewers to know which of those two responses will be the most appropriate. Because the range of unscripted questions is so wide there is no real way to guess them in advance but below are a few of those that some big companies have employed and studying them will give you a taste of what you might come up against. Remember that the questioner is using them to get a look at you as a person so you need to use these as a chance to show your stuff. Maintain your physical posture, eye contact and general poise at all times. If you are flustered just make sure they don't know that.

Pretend you are our CEO. What three concerns about the firm's future will keep you up at night?

This question gives you a chance to both show that you have really researched the company to whom you are applying as well as offer some positive sounding future plans. Don't let it look like you have all the answers or that you are afraid that there are intrinsic problems in the company that really concern you. (Vault)

Why are manhole covers round?

If you happen to be a bit on the rotund side then this is the time to show you have a little humor and can laugh at yourself by suggesting that it allows easier access to rounder physiques like your own. Make sure that you bear the brunt of the joke and do not aim it at overweight city workers. If your physique does not open a door for this sort of humor then try suggesting that most of the holes are round and so it makes sense to have a cover that fits. (Google)

What's your favorite song? Perform it for us now.

This question is not to see if you can sing and 'I did it My Way' is the wrong answer. On the other hand 'Love me Do' by the Beatles might raise a smile and it's easy enough to sing to. (Living social)

Any advice for your previous boss?

You are on dangerous ground here. Pointing out your ex boss's weak points are not what the interviewer is hoping to see. 'Good luck with finding the three new staff you will need to replace me.' might work. (Quora)

How would you solve problems if you were from Mars?

"I have the technology, intelligence and capability to come all the way from Mars. You are the ones with a problem. How are you going to deal with me?" (Amazon)

How would you rate your memory?

"I used to know the answer to that one I'm sure. Can you give me a few minutes to think about it?" Now move in with examples of why your memory is actually good. (Glassdoor)

What's the color of money?

Slightly darker than water but it runs through your fingers more easily. (American Heart Association)

You are a new addition to a crayon box. What color are you?

"A sort embarrassed red color but I will pale down to a more typical flesh color when I have become more used to being in this new environment. (Urban Outfitters)

What do you think about when you alone in your car?

"For the past two weeks I thought about possible questions I might need to be prepared for during this interview. Clearly I did not think broadly enough because that was a question I had not considered. However I did think of these points to show why I am the ideal candidate...." and then take the floor by presenting some of the reasons you should have the job. (Gallop)

How many balloons would fit in this room?

Cast an eye around the room and then ask if the furniture is to be removed first. Whichever way they answer you then reply "11927 providing they were fully inflated." Nobody can argue with you because they have no idea. (Price Waterhouse Coopers)

As you can see the range of unscripted questions is endless and there is no real way you can anticipate what they might be. Instead use them as an opportunity to show those sides of your character such as wit, humor, quick thinking ability and the ability not to get flustered under pressure. That is what you are being tested for with these sorts of questions. You will need to be creative enough to develop your own answers and you will need to be confident enough to do so on the spur of the moment. The main point of this chapter is not to provide answers but to demonstrate that just as the questions are out of the box, so too can your answers be.

Strategies and Techniques

In the following chapters I'm going to share with you a few interview techniques that will give an added level of confidence that not knowing the best answers to interview questions may not give you.

Have you ever studied hard for a test then froze up when it came to give your answers? Or perhaps, you prepared for a speech and you forgot what you were going to say? You may know the perfect answers to the toughest interview questions, but if you don't get rid of the fear of screwing it up the perfect answers will leave you tongue-tied!

The following chapters contain proven steps and strategies on how to prepare mentally for your interview. It'll give you tips and techniques on how to manage pre-interview anxiety and stress, on how to keep, maintain, and show your emotional confidence, how to think on your feet and give impromptu yet intelligent answers. I have also given a few insights on how to handle a couple of tricky situations and/or questions that usually raise their ugly head during an interview.

Being clever and having sufficient knowledge in your domain is not enough for success in your career. Great communication skills, people management skills, ability to think out-of-the-box, being open-minded, and your willingness to correct yourself, and additional soft skills are equally important for making a successful career.

Before you go on, I'd like to ask you for a favor. I want to reach as many people as I can with this book and if you agree with what you have read so far then I'd like to ask you to leave a review on Amazon by clicking the link below. By leaving a review you are helping me to achieve that goal!

Click This Link to Leave a Review On Amazon!

Thank you for taking the time as many who found this book helpful left reviews. Now back to preparing you for your interview.

Chapter 7:

How to Manage Pre-Interview Anxiety Issues

While it is almost impossible to avoid "feeling" anxious before an important job interview, it is definitely possible and perhaps easy to manage this stress and keep it from reflecting in your behavior and attitude. When you appear anxious, your interviewers feel put off; it sends a negative signal that makes them think that if you cannot handle interview pressure then how can you handle bigger pressures in the organization. Anxiety can put off interviewers quickly.

However, you cannot really stop feeling anxious! You can manage the way it shows on your face, your body language, your tone of voice, and your choice of words. Moreover, anxiety is contagious; the resultant negativity flows to the interviewers and they become as confused as you and the only loser in this entire process is you; they are bound to find someone else for their organization. Hence, remember, it is perfectly natural to feel anxious but you have to learn not to show anxiety.

The following tips will help you manage anxiety and prevent it from deterring your career:

- **Overview** - Get an overview of the place of interview. Visit it beforehand so that you do not waste precious resources and enhance anxiety trying to find it on the day of the interview.
- **Reach ahead of time** - Reach the designated interview place at least 15 minutes before the interview. This gives you time to catch your breath, to collect yourself, visit the restroom if needed, get a last-minute look at yourself to see if something is amiss, and other such small yet very important details.
- **Update your domain skills** - Make sure you do your homework for the interview with regards to your domain

knowledge. Ensure you brush up your skills and your mind is sharp and updated with the latest happenings in your field.

- **Research about the company** - Ensure you research the company thoroughly. Know everything about the company; know in detail about the position you have applied for. You can gather ample information from a host of sources including but not limited to the Internet, magazines, the company website, blogs, and more. Speak to industry insiders and maybe to friends who are working there already. The more data you have the more armed and less anxious you are.

- **Know your interviewer** - Try and see if you can find out who is going to conduct the interview. Will it be someone from HR? Will it be a domain expert from the company? Will there be more than one interviewer? Knowing this information helps you prepare better.

- **Keep an impeccable appearance** - Ensure your attire and demeanor match that of the company. Ensure your clothes are clean, neatly pressed, and are a good fit for you. Try and avoid clothes that are too loud. A formal appearance is better than an informal one as it adds a sense of professionalism to your overall attitude. Again, it might make sense to visit the place and see how the existing employees turn out for work.

- **Rest, exercise, and food** - Sleep well the night before and include a small physical routine on the morning of the interview. Definitely, eat something. This helps in keeping your mind and body sharp, active, and alert.

- **List questions** - Make a list of likely questions; prepare answers for them and practice saying the responses in front of the mirror. You will then know if your verbal and non-verbal communications are in sync with each other. Practicing aloud also helps you control the tone and the texture of your voice.

- **Know yourself better** - Know your strengths and weaknesses. Be proud (not arrogant) about your strengths; humbly acknowledge your weaknesses; however, have ready answers for how you plan to either overcome or work around your limitations. Avoid making excuses for your weaknesses. This attitude reflects a very strong personality.

- **Match your strength with what the company wants** - Prepare answers that reflect what you can offer to the company specifically. This requires a lot of preparation, as you will have to sit down and match your strengths with what the company is looking for in their candidate and then give appropriate responses in the interview.

- **Eye contact** - Make eye contact with your interviewer(s) while you are talking.

- **Take time off to think** - It is perfectly fine to think before you answer. This is an interview and not a rapid-fire question round. Thinking gives you time for framing sentences correctly, controlling your breath, getting the right tone and texture for your voice and more. Even while you are responding, feel free to pause and think before adding something more, making you look like a person who thinks well before doing or saying something.

- **Keep panic and desperation away** - Do not panic and take measures that come across as desperate. Maintain your dignity. Let this reflect in the way you sit, in the way you talk, in your seemingly calm facial expressions and more.

- **Show a balanced attitude** - While enthusiasm is good, remember not to go overboard. Over-enthusiasm could also be seen as anxiety or fear. It might present a message that you are so stressed out that you will do anything to get this job. This is definitely not a good sign for the interviewers to see.

- **Happy perspectives** - Visualize an interview wherein both you and the interviewers are smiling and happy. This happy disposition is a great confidence booster.

And before I end this chapter, I want to reiterate multiple times: Prepare! Prepare! Prepare! There is nothing like being as prepared as possible to lower anxiety and help you manage interview-related stress. The more prepared you are the less anxious you will appear! There is no shortcut for preparation. Hard work, diligence, and a sense of commitment are absolutely necessary tools to achieve success from the beginning of the career.

Chapter 8:

Thinking on Your Feet

While many of the challenges of a job interview can be handled by preparing, there will invariably be situations that require you to extempore. Getting stumped for an answer and the sense of bewilderment on your face can cost you your dream job. Hence, along with preparing well, you have to pick up skills of "thinking on your feet" or coming up with something smart, intelligent and witty at the spur of the moment.

Here are some tips to help you hone "thinking on your feet" skills:

Do not jump to give answers; think before responding: Thinking on your feet is exactly that, "think" and then answer. Answers need not come out of your mouth at the speed of light. Answers have to be sensible, practical, truthful, and perhaps witty.

Slow down: If you believe you are giving in to pressure, relax and slow down your thinking and talking speed. Remember you are not under any obligation to give brilliant answers at the drop of a hat. Slacken your pace, say something sensible, and allow your mind and body time to come out of the "pressure" situation.

Prepare well for common questions that will definitely be asked: Ensure you do not keep everything under the "thinking on your feet" category. In fact, most questions will need preparation. Only a very small portion of questions will perhaps require thinking on your feet. So please prepare.

Use storytelling strategies: Without hurting anyone's sentiments, use stories to bring in some sunshine and wit into the interview session. For this, keep a few amusing anecdotes from your life experiences that you would like to share. This can definitely lighten the mood and change the way you are perceived by the interviewers. However, take care not to get frivolous with your attitude.

Do not hesitate to ask for time: Instead of sounding wrong or even worse, stupid by giving inappropriate answers, a much better option would be to ask for time. Answers like, "Can I answer that just before the interview finishes? I need to think the responses through," would be great. Request them for the next question but remember to come back and give your answer for the one you had taken time.

Relaxing techniques: When you begin to feel the pressure take deep breaths, clench and unclench invisible muscles like feet, thighs, and biceps. This relaxes you and helps you release the pressure you are feeling. Then take a few seconds and give affirming responses.

Listening and observation skills: If you practice enough, many times you will see that answers are hidden in the question itself and/or in the body language of the interviewer. It requires acute listening and observation skills to get the meaning of the words and gestures used. For example, the interviewer might be deliberately asking you for a non-existent answer. The words may not convey this. However, there could be an imperceptible twinkle in his or her eye giving you the indication that he or she is checking how far you will go. This realization releases stress immediately and more often than not you will come up with something smart.

Ask for the question to be repeated: While this is an excellent tactic to get more time to think, many times the repetition of the question gives you an opportunity to see a new meaning in it. This new perspective that you missed the first time the question was asked could give you the help needed to answer it appropriately. Moreover, when you ask for the question to be repeated you are giving the impression that you are keen on fully understanding the query before venturing to answer.

Stalling Tactics: Many times the pressure you feel to answer a question is because you think there is not enough time to ponder. This is not true at all. You can use stalling tactics to give yourself the time needed to think. One way is to repeat the question yourself thus giving you the opportunity to clarify, a positive reflection of your personality and, of course, more time.

Sometimes, narrowing the focus of the question is a good stalling tactic. For example, you could reframe the question like this: "You asked about the impact of my idea on customers? Do you mean in terms of service or in terms of product availability?" Such tangential cross questions give the impression that you definitely know your subject well.

The above are some tips that will help you improve your "thinking on your feet" skills. However, like most things in the world, mastering requires a lot of practice and hard work. Do not hesitate to do that.

Thinking on your feet is an excellent skill to learn and master, as it will help your perceived image get a huge makeover. The astute, clever, and honest responses you give will instill confidence among the interviewers and enhance your chances of landing your dream job multifold.

Chapter 9:

Emotional Confidence

It is an accepted fact that just academic and professional excellence is merely not enough to get you a good job. This also means all toppers in academics need not land themselves their dream job. A successful interviewee is the one who has an improved emotional quotient and better people management skills.

Emotional intelligence or emotional confidence is based on your ability to know, understand, and leverage human emotions positively. If your emotional intelligence is high, then you will be able to:

- Recognize the emotional status of others as well as your own
- Engage with people such that they are drawn to you
- Easily discern emotional cues that will help you communicate effectively. This will help you build strong relationship with people

Find common emotional connections between the interviewer(s) and yourself: Finding these human connections clears the way for a smooth interview. Because there are common emotions involved you will feel more confident and less intimidated during the interview. Here are some tips to find out what you and the others in the interview room have in common:

Research and prepare: If you know who the interviewer(s) are, then find out beforehand their likes and dislikes. Subtly and imperceptibly, see if you can bring up the topic during the interview. I am sure the people involved will perk up and listen to your responses better.

Listen well: While simply listening well during the course you are bound to find a few emotional commonalities. During the conversation, if the interviewer mentions his or her alma mater, or his or her family weekend, or his or her favorite sport or book or actor, you could have the presence of mind to lead the topic gradually in that direction without seeming to be in control of the actual interview. An emotional bond between you and the interviewer(s) is automatically set up.

However, handle this aspect with care because if there is more than one interviewer, you do run the risk of antagonizing the other unwittingly.

Start talking about your own passions and interests: If nothing worthwhile (at least from an emotional perspective) is coming up, then do not hesitate to talk about your own passions and interests. And if these interests are true, then the emotional angle will definitely come forth. It might make sense to think of using things that are trending; for example, a book that has caught the attention of the world; you could state what you feel and say positive things. It is prudent to keep out negativities when trying to establish an emotional connection.

While you are trying to keep that emotional confidence of yours high and attempting to connect with one or more of the interviewers, do not to pummel them with questions. Remember, you are NOT the interviewer! Let the conversation flow happen as naturally as you can and any additions from your side should not appear forced.

How to appear confident during an interview

Here are a few tips to build confidence during your interview process:

Take deep breaths: This technique helps you relax and release all stress hormones giving you the much-needed confidence boost.

Avoid fidgeting: Be mindful of where your hands are placed. Do not play with your fingers or fidget around with something on the table or near you. These are sure shot symptoms of nervousness, which your interviewers will catch and get put off by. Place your hands and legs in a comfortable position. If during the interview you have to get up and move and then return to your seat, remember to get back to that same comfortable yet formal posture.

Slow down your talking speed: Rambling is another clear symptom of nervousness. Be consciousness of what you are saying and talk slowly and with deliberation. Take one thought at a time, use the correct words to present this thought and then move on to the next thought. Be mindful of how fast or how slow you are talking.

Positive thinking: There is nothing like positive thoughts to boost your confidence. Think of an event where you won a prize; a debate where your speech was greatly applauded; a play in which you played a role in either in school or college and remember those happy moments. These happy thoughts will trigger confidence in you by reducing stress and anxiety

So relax, slow down, gather strength, and above all, prepare well!

Chapter 10:

How to Handle Sticky Situations

Job interviews are by themselves very unnerving; however, the bad news, sometimes, does not end there. There could arise a few really sticky situations wherein you feel stumped, lost, and completely addled and you simply cannot find a way out of the mess. This chapter is dedicated to a few such sticky situations and how you can manage them.

The Unprofessional Interviewer

Yes, there are many unprofessional people working in large corporate houses and you could find yourself being interviewed by one of them. These people normally are not great interviewers and/or enjoy needling the interviewees. In addition, your interviewer could be unfocused, completely detached, disinterested and worse, totally unprepared and perhaps, does not even have your resume handy let alone having read it.

For such people and situations, do not hesitate to hand over a copy of your resume at the start with a polite question such as, "Can I take you through my professional career?" Yes, in these cases, you will be leading the interview; at least in the beginning till, hopefully, your interviewer gets his hand on what he or she wants to do.

A bigmouth interviewer will be talking so much that you will never get the opportunity or chance to say anything worthwhile. Such times do not hesitate to lean forward, open your mouth gesturing that you want to say something and even the most talkative person is bound to ask your opinion. At this juncture, you could speak about strengths and how it can help the organization.

Tell me about yourself

Despite this question being a very commonly asked one, it has the power to rattle and unnerve interviewees. The preparation will definitely help in most cases. Be succinct, crisp, and clear. Create a small summary combining your personal and professional life till then and present it confidently.

Use those specific strengths of yours that are called for in the job position and do not hesitate to sell yourself proudly (not arrogantly). Choose only those points that are relevant to the job and do NOT make your answer long, elaborate, and downright boring.

Questions that have "no right answer"

These offbeat questions are usually targeted at you to check how well you are able to think on your feet. Remember, weird though they may seem, your responses to these questions reflect your core personality. So be extremely careful about how you answer them. An example of such a question: If you were given an opportunity to turn into a beast, which would you choose and why?

There are no right answers and every answer has its own merits and demerits. Do not be unnerved by these kinds of queries. Take a minute to gather your thoughts and be assured something will pop in your head because you are already well prepared. However, be honest and do not exaggerate to the point of complete disbelief and this attitude reflects on your casual approach to most things in life. Be realistic and come up with answers that are logical and make sense.

Another inevitable "no-right-answer" question is "where do you see yourself five years from now?" The answer for this is entirely dependent on the company and the position you have applied for. While some companies and/or positions need ambitious people others may want ambitions in moderation. Since you have already researched about the company and the job position, work on the best answer for this question and come prepared.

Questions about salary

If this question comes too early on, then this could mean that if you quote a figure too high or too low, the interview will quickly call the meeting to an end as he or she does not want to waste time. However, a good response to the salary question could be: I applied for the post because the job description intrigued me and I believe it is a perfect fit for the set of skills that I have acquired. So, can we postpone the salary question till we are sure that I am a good fit for the job?

Questions about earlier terminations

These extremely sticky questions have the power to make you squirm. However, be aware of these negative feelings and respond objectively. Never lie about anything but also remember not to speak too much about it. List your reasons objectively and end by say, "As the company and I were not a good fit, we parted ways."

Personal Questions

I believe that a good way to handle uncomfortable relationship-based personal questions is by firmly yet gently saying, "No matter what personal problems or issues I may have, I will never allow them to come in the way of my job."

Each job interview is unique and has to be handled differently. Remember that sticky situations and people are all around you. They are there in your personal life as well as your professional life. You, more often than not, find ways and means to mitigate the stickiness and unpleasantness around you. The skills that you use in your life to manage difficult situations and people are the same skills that are required to handle a job interview, the only difference being the level of professionalism and formality involved.

Conclusion:

Your Turn to Ask

There is any number of variations to all interview questions, but if you have ready answers to all of the above then it is unlikely that you will find yourself caught off balance. Hopefully you have learned that preparation and research are fundamental to interview success. The interview is an amalgamation of dress, demeanor, body language and charisma but even should you have been gifted with a natural abundance of all of those things, failure to prepare can let you down.

Try not to see the interviewer as someone whose job it is to stop you getting employed in his company. He wants you to get the job. Hiring the right people is his business and obviously you see yourself as the right person. As you will have seen in the list of questions in the previous chapter, many of them appear difficult but can be turned into positive opportunities to shine a light on your attributes if you are prepared for them. The masters of turning questions around are politicians and you can learn a great deal by watching them handle difficult interviews. Over the years they become very adept at taking difficult questions and transforming them into opportunities to get their message across. You need to start looking at each question and seeing how you can use it as a way to show the interviewer that you are both human and capable of doing the work he wants done.

Once you have been put through the interview process a good interviewer should give you the opportunity to ask some questions of your own. If he does not provide you with that opportunity then do not be shy to ask for it. The interviewer has a right to learn as much about you as he can but you have just as much right to find out as much as you can about the job and what will be expected of you. Don't be intimidated here. You are not being impolite or too demanding if you make some simple enquiries as to the exact parameters of the job you will be required to perform. The interviewer should, if he is worth his salt, appreciate that you want a full job description and should be happy to give it to you. If he is not, that should raise alarm bells.

Once again your research is going to come to the fore here. Hopefully you have a fairly clear idea of what the company is about and what their ethos is. After a long interview you do not want to reveal a blind spot in the information you have, nor do you want to waste the interviewers time explaining basic facts that you could easily have picked up yourself.

What you do need to do is clarify exactly what the remuneration package is and check that there will be no hidden deductions of any kind. If it has not already been made clear then you will want precise details as to working hours, working conditions and vacations. The interviewer should have this information at his fingertips and should be willing to share it with you readily. Do not be put off with the attitude that all those minor details can be sorted out once you have started work. It is preferable that both parties are fully conversant with what they expect of one another right from the start.

In your research you may have turned up some details you are unclear about. For example you may have read that there could be an impending buy out by another company. You need to find out if that will affect you and if so how. Don't retreat from asking these sorts of questions just because you are the one being interviewed here. Your future is at stake and you are well within your rights to get some clarification. If anything, it should demonstrate to the interviewer that you have done your research and that you have gone out of your way to find out about the company.

Once you have had all your queries satisfactorily answered then the interview should come to an end. Be sure to finish off on a good note. Thank the interviewer for giving you the opportunity to try out for the position and ask if there is any further information that he needs. Keep your body language positive, give a firm handshake and mention that you look forward to hearing from them in the near future. If you can you should try to establish when you will be notified as to whether or not your application has been successful as you don't want to be left hanging in limbo. Don't forget to smile!

BONUS: Free Interview Coaching

By purchasing your copy of *Interview: Best Answers to Tough Questions for Total Confidence* you may now book your 30-minute complimentary coaching session with a Certified Professional Coach by visiting the link below.

https://coachmenow.youcanbook.me/

I Need Your Help...

I really want to thank you for reading this book. I sincerely hope you received valuable insights and guidance to land you perfect job.

This is some of the best compellation of work on not only preparing answers to questions but also having the inner readiness for a confident interview I have put together.

People who have found my book helpful left a kind review on Amazon. I want to reach as many people with this book as possible. By leaving a review you are helping me to accomplish that! Please leave an honest review of you purchase on Amazon.com

Thank you for your time. I wish you the best of luck and blessings in your new position!

www.ingramcontent.com/pod-product-compliance
Lightning Source LLC
Chambersburg PA
CBHW061229180526
45170CB00003B/1221